The
Guit
Scale Book

by Darryl Winston.

ver 100 essential scales for the contemporary guitarist.
Fully fingered in standard notation and tablature.

Amsco Publications
New York • London • Sydney

Interior design and layout by Amy Appleby and Peter Picko
Music engraving by Chelsea Music Engraving

Order No. AM 91462
US International Standard Book Number: 0.8256.1370.1
UK International Standard Book Number: 0.7119.3699.4

Exclusive Distributors:
Music Sales Corporation
257 Park Avenue South, New York, NY 10010 USA
Music Sales Limited
8/9 Frith Street, London W1V 5TZ England
Music Sales Pty. Limited
120 Rothschild Street, Rosebery, Sydney, NSW 2018, Austra

Printed in the United States of America by
Vicks Lithograph and Printing Corporation

Table of Contents

Introduction

Regular scale practice is a sure way to improve your playing ability—and this book contains over 100 useful scales for the advanced guitarist. You can use this material to develop your playing skills is a variety of different ways. Rock, jazz, and blues guitarists study scales to find new sources for improvising solos and writing songs. Others practice advanced scales to improve their ability to transpose music into different modes and keys. Some guitarists simply wish to build strength and coordination in both hands—and add confidence and polish to their overall performance style. Whatever your focus, you will find that mastering advanced scales will improve your ability to play music in all styles—from classical to rock.

This book includes a wide range of scale forms and professional fingerings, provided in music notation and guitar tablature. Many scales in this book are used in blues, jazz, and rock improvisation, while some are identified more frequently with folk and classical music. Certain scales are specifically designed to improve the advanced player's strength and facility across the length of the fretboard. Other advanced scales involve special techniques, such as tap-ons, harmonics, or the use of open strings. For those interested in progressive and "world" musics, there are also some fascinating exotic scales from Africa, Eastern Europe, India, Malaysia, and Japan.

You will find a wealth of scales in this book for use in practice and performance—and a lifetime of source material for composing your own music and solo parts. You can practice these scales in any order you wish—or simply use this book as a reference for scales and fingerings as needed. Remember, even the most advanced player will benefit greatly from practicing scales—even after they have become "old friends."

Moveable Major Scales

Guitarists refer to certain scale patterns as *moveable scales* because they can simply "move" the pattern to a new position on the fretboard to play the same scale in another key. In this section, you'll practice seven different fingering patterns used to play major scales in every key. These patterns are also the models for many of the modal and advanced scales introduced later in this book. Take the time to memorize these seven important fingering patterns so that you will be able to easily adapt them to a wide range of scale forms.

Play each of these fingering types now as shown below in second position. Some of the fingering types require that you *stretch* your first or fourth fretting finger down or up one fret to reach a note (indicated by an *s*).

Type 1

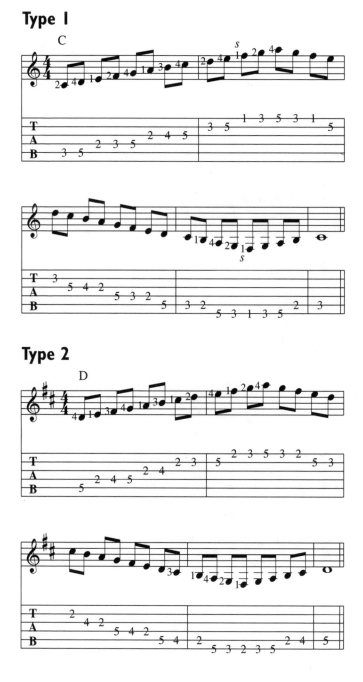

Type 2

Type 3

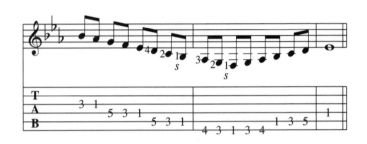

Type 4

Type 5

Type 6

Type 7

These seven fingering types allow for seven alternatives for playing a major scale in each of the twelve keys.

Major Scale Positions

Key	Fingering Type						
	1	2	3	4	5	6	7
C	II	XII	XI	IX	VII	V	IV
D♭ (C♯)	III	I	XII	X	VIII	VI	V
D	IV	II	XIII	XI	IX	VII	VI
E♭	V	III	II	XII	X	VIII	VII
E	VI	IV	III	XIII	XI	IX	VIII
F	VII	V	IV	II	XII	X	IX
G♭ (F♯)	VIII	VI	V	III	I	XI	X
G	IX	VII	VI	IV	II	XII	XI
A♭	X	VIII	VII	V	III	I	XII
A	XI	IX	VIII	VI	IV	II	XIII
B♭	XII	X	IX	VII	V	III	II
B (C♭)	XIII	XI	X	VIII	VI	IV	III

The following major-scale pattern incorporates all seven fingering types in the key of C. Repeat this exercise several times at a moderate tempo. As you play, notice how you must shift up the neck for each new fingering type. Once you can play the whole pattern smoothly and evenly from memory, try playing it again several times at a relatively fast tempo for a real workout.

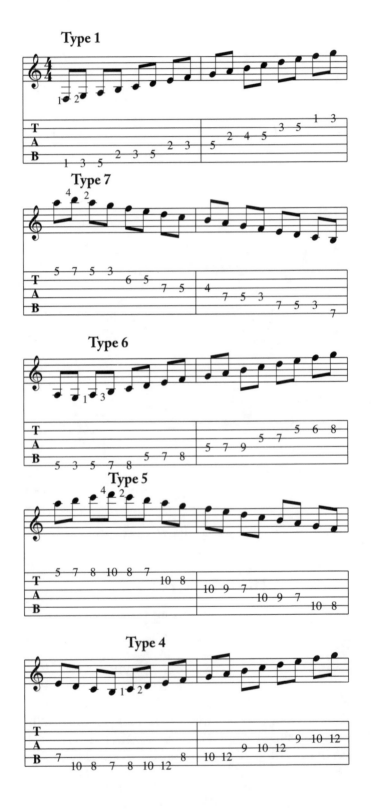

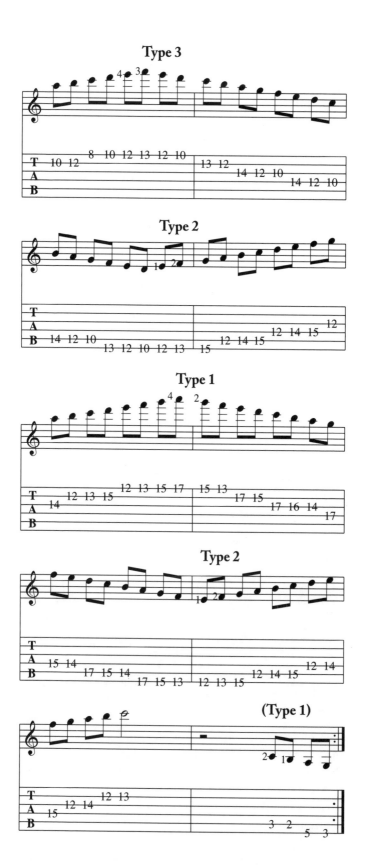

As you can see, these fingering types allow you to play a C major scale just about anywhere on the guitar fretboard. Once you know this exercise well, use the chart on page 9 to create similar major-scale patterns in other keys.

Modulating Major Scales

The *circle of fifths* provides a useful pattern for practicing an extended scale pattern that *modulates* through all twelve keys. You can use this pattern (and variations on it) to practice many types of advanced scales using the full range of the fretboard. The circle of fifths begins with the key of C major, progresses clockwise through the twelve major keys, then returns to the key of C. Note that certain keys share a position on the circle of fifths (B/C♭, F♯/G♭, and C♯/D♭). The keys within each pair are called *enharmonic equivalents*—thus, B major is the enharmonic equivalent of C♭ major, and vice versa. Although these two scales sound exactly alike, they are notated as different keys (depending on the harmonic context of a particular piece of music). To avoid repetition, the most commonly used scale of each enharmonic pair is presented in the scale exercises that follow.

Circle of Fifths

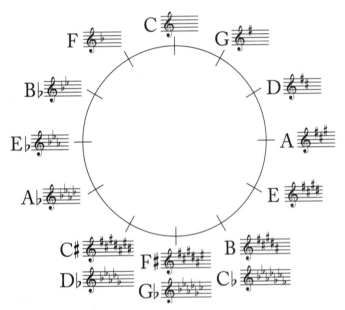

The circle of fifths provides the blueprint for this modulating major scale, which begins in the key of C and ends in the key of F. Once you are familiar with this scale, try creating your own variations on this pattern by starting in a key other than C—or by varying fingering types (or positions).

C Major (Type 1)

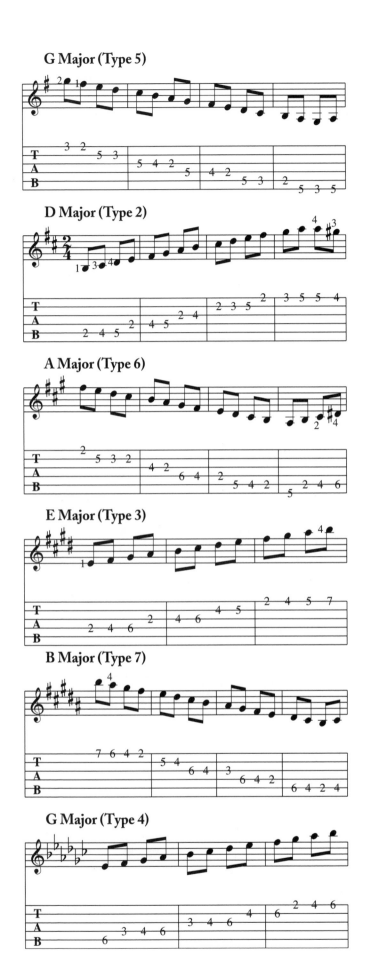

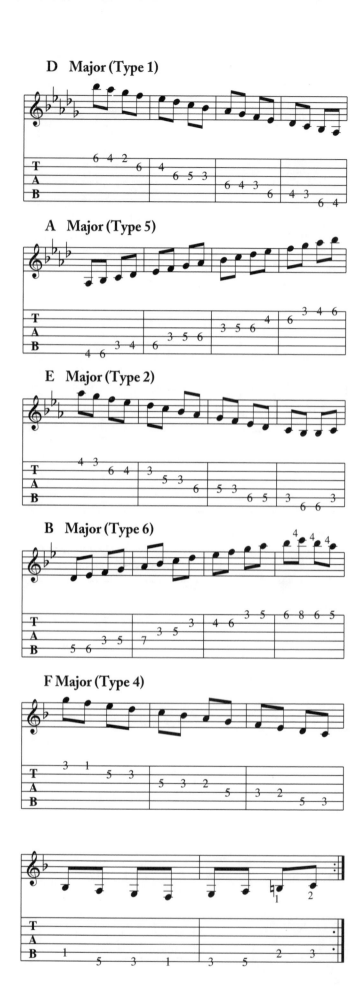

The Modes

Derived from the modes of Ancient Greece, the modern modes were actually developed in the 9th century as the basis for Gregorian chant and other religious music. In 19th and 20th century classical music, these modes are used to invoke the mood of 16th century sacred music—or to express the ethnic flavor of Slavic and other folk musics characterized by modal tonalities. In modern rock, jazz, pop, and new age music, modes are used to add drama and ambiance to songs and instrumentals. In fact, today's composers often draw upon the modes to create new and interesting tonalities using these relatively ancient sources.

Understanding and mastering modal scales will help the advanced guitarist perform in a variety of musical styles. Heavy metal and experimental rock music draw heavily on the modes to achieve an innovative and powerful sound. For the rock and jazz guitarist, modal scales provide a rich source for improvisational ideas for both solos and accompaniments. Modes also occur in a wide range of classical and folk musics of different cultures (and in contemporary music that imitates these genres).

A modal scale is formed by displacing the first note of a given scale without changing its interval formula. Although modes may be derived from any scale, the seven standard or *authentic modes* are built upon the major scale. Below is a brief description of the seven basic modes and their common uses in modern music.

The Ionian Scale. This is actually an alternative name for the major scale, discussed previously. As you will see in the sections that follow, all of the other modes are derived from the Ionian scale.

The Dorian Scale. Begins on the second degree of the major scale. This scale resembles the natural minor scale with a raised sixth. A decided favorite of today's jazz and rock guitarists, the Dorian scale is particularly useful for improvised solos over minor seventh, minor ninth, and minor thirteenth chords.

The Phrygian Scale. Begins on the third degree of the major scale. This scale resembles the natural minor scale with a lowered second. In early music, this mode was used to create a solemn quality—and it is sometimes used for this same purpose in rock and heavy metal music today. The Phrygian mode is also used to add a distinctive Latin flavor to pop and rock music, where it is useful for improvised solos over minor seventh and minor ninth chords.

The Lydian Scale. Begins on the fourth degree of the major scale. This scale has a major sound, but with a raised fourth (or *tritone*). The Lydian mode is used in jazz music over major seventh chords (with the exception of the I chord). An altered version of this scale, the *Lydian flat-seven*, is discussed later in the book.

The Mixolydian Scale. Begins on the fifth degree of the major scale. Like the Lydian scale, the Mixolydian scale has a major sound (except that its seventh degree is lowered). You can hear the Mixolydian mode in many folk and rock tunes. It is useful for improvised lines with dominant seventh, dominant ninth, and dominant thirteenth chords.

The Aeolian Scale. Also called the *natural minor scale*, this scale begins on the sixth degree of the major scale. Because it is a true minor key, the Aeolian mode is considered to be the relative minor of the major key from which it is derived. The Aeolian mode is widely used in popular music of all kinds—from pop-rock to heavy metal. This scale works well with minor seventh, minor ninth, minor eleventh, and minor thirteenth chords.

The Locrian Scale. Begins on the seventh degree of the major scale. Since it is built around a diminished triad, it has somewhat limited use. However, you will sometimes hear a jazz guitarist use this scale when soloing over a minor seventh ♭5 (half-diminished) chord.

Below are the seven modal scales that are derived from the C major scale.

C Ionian (or C Major) Scale

D Dorian Scale

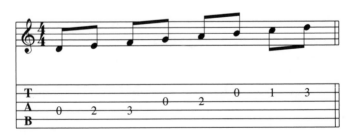

E Phrygian Scale

F Lydian Scale

G Mixolydian Scale

A Aeolian (or A Natural Minor) Scale

B Locrian Scale

Parallel Modal Scales

The seven modal scales that share the same starting note (or *tonic*) are called *parallel modal scales*. For example, A Dorian is a parallel modal scale of A Phrygian. The seven parallel modes of any given tonic are derived from seven different major scales. Take a look at the major scales used to produce the seven parallel modal scales that begin on an A note.

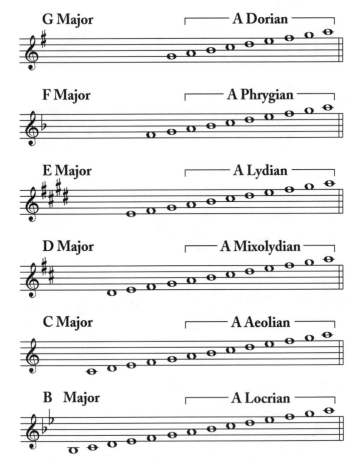

The scale pattern that follows features the seven parallel modes that begin on an A note. Notice that the key signature changes with each new mode.

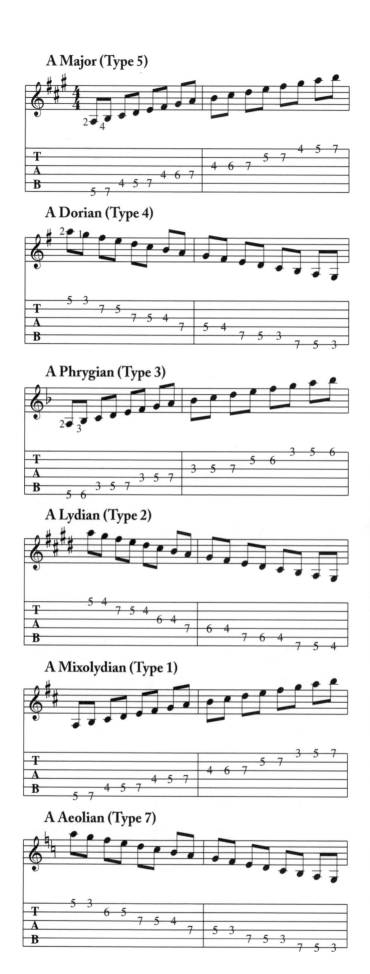

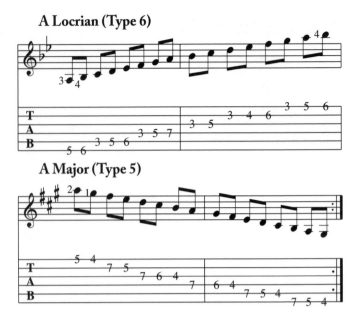

A Locrian (Type 6)

A Major (Type 5)

Once you are familiar with this scale pattern, play it again using a different tonic note to explore seven parallel modes in a new key. (Just refer to the following section, "Transposing Modal Scales," to determine the key signature, position, and fingering type to use for any given modal scale.)

For example, here's how you would begin a one-octave version of the same pattern for the seven parallel modes that begin on an E note.

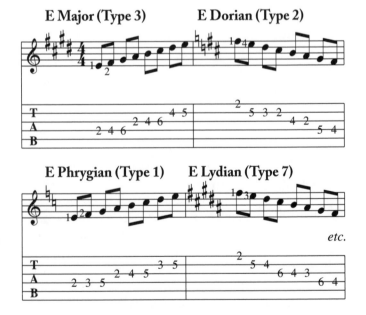

E Major (Type 3)   **E Dorian (Type 2)**

E Phrygian (Type 1)   **E Lydian (Type 7)**

etc.

Transposing Modal Scales

The chart below allows you to find the key signature for any mode. So, to play a C Dorian scale, begin on a C note, but use the key signature of B♭ (two flats). Or, to play a B♯ Locrian scale, start on B♯, but use the key signature of C♯. Enharmonic equivalents are linked by brackets at the left. Note that some of these key signatures are used for fewer than six modal scales.

Key Signatures for Modes
(Shows the major key signature for each mode in every key)

	Dorian	Phrygian	Lydian	Mixolydian	Aeolian	Locrian
⌈ B♯	—	—	—	—	—	C♯
⌊ C	B♭	A♭	G	F	E♭	D♭
⌈ C♯	B	A	—	F♯	E	D
⌊ D♭	C♭	—	A♭	G♭	—	—
D	C	B♭	A	G	F	E♭
⌈ D♯	C♯	B	—	—	F♯	E
⌊ E♭	D♭	C♭	B♭	A♭	G♭	—
⌈ E	D	C	B	A	G	F
⌊ F♭	—	—	C♭	—	—	—
⌈ E♯	—	C♯	—	—	—	F♯
⌊ F	E♭	D♭	C	B♭	A♭	G♭
⌈ F♯	E	D	C♯	B	A	G
⌊ G♭	—	—	D♭	C♭	—	—
G	F	E♭	D	C	B♭	A♭
⌈ G♯	F♯	E	—	C♯	B	A
⌊ A♭	G♭	—	E♭	D♭	C♭	—
A	G	F	E	D	C	B♭
⌈ A♯	—	F♯	—	—	C♯	B
⌊ B♭	A♭	G♭	F	E♭	D♭	C♭
⌈ B	A	G	F♯	E	D	C
⌊ C♭	—	—	G♭	—	—	—

Since the modes are derived from major scales, you can use the seven major-scale fingering types to play modal scales. The charts that follow provide the position and fingering type used to play scales in every modal key. Take the time to develop your own modal scale patterns using the charts in this section. This will improve your ability to transpose modal scales on the spot—and to improvise freely using these interesting and evocative scale forms.

Dorian Scale Positions

Key	Fingering Type						
	1	2	3	4	5	6	7
C	XII	X	IX	VII	V	III	II
C♯ (D♭)	XIII	XI	X	VIII	VI	IV	III
D	II	XII	XI	IX	VII	V	IV
E♭ (D♯)	III	I	XII	X	VIII	VI	V
E	IV	II	XIII	XI	IX	VII	VI
F	V	III	II	XII	X	VIII	VII
F♯	VI	IV	III	XIII	XI	IX	VIII
G	VII	V	IV	II	XII	X	IX
A♭ (G♯)	VIII	VI	V	III	I	XI	X
A	IX	VII	VI	IV	II	XII	XI
B♭	X	VIII	VII	V	III	I	XII
B	XI	IX	VIII	VI	IV	II	XIII

Phrygian Scale Positions

Key	Fingering Type						
	1	2	3	4	5	6	7
C	X	VIII	VII	V	III	I	XII
C♯	XI	IX	VIII	VI	IV	II	XIII
D	XII	X	IX	VII	V	III	II
E♭ (D♯)	XIII	XI	X	VIII	VI	IV	III
E	II	XII	XI	IX	VII	V	IV
F (E♯)	III	I	XII	X	VIII	VI	V
F♯	IV	II	XIII	XI	IX	VII	VI
G	V	III	II	XII	X	VIII	VII
G♯	VI	IV	III	XIII	XI	IX	VIII
A	VII	V	IV	II	XII	X	IX
B♭ (A♯)	VIII	VI	V	III	I	XI	X
B	IX	VII	VI	IV	II	XII	XI

Lydian Scale Positions

Key	Fingering Type						
	1	2	3	4	5	6	7
C	IX	VII	VI	IV	II	XII	XI
D♭	X	VIII	VII	V	III	I	XII
D	XI	IX	VIII	VI	IV	II	XIII
E♭	XII	X	IX	VII	V	III	II
E (F♭)	XIII	XI	X	VIII	VI	IV	III
F	II	XII	XI	IX	VII	V	IV
G♭ (F♯)	III	I	XII	X	VIII	VI	V
G	IV	II	XIII	XI	IX	VII	VI
A♭	V	III	II	XII	X	VIII	VII
A	VI	IV	III	XIII	XI	IX	VIII
B♭	VII	V	IV	II	XII	X	IX
C♭ (B)	VIII	VI	V	III	I	XI	X

Mixolydian Scale Positions

Key	Fingering Type						
	1	2	3	4	5	6	7
C	VII	V	IV	II	XII	X	IX
Db (C#)	VIII	VI	V	III	I	XI	X
D	IX	VII	VI	IV	II	XII	XI
Eb	X	VIII	VII	V	III	I	XII
E	XI	IX	VIII	VI	IV	II	XIII
F	XII	X	IX	VII	V	III	II
F# (Gb)	XIII	XI	X	VIII	VI	IV	III
G	II	XII	XI	IX	VII	V	IV
Ab (G#)	III	I	XII	X	VIII	VI	V
A	IV	II	XIII	XI	IX	VII	VI
Bb	V	III	II	XII	X	VIII	VII
B	VI	IV	III	XIII	XI	IX	VIII

Aeolian Scale Positions

Key	Fingering Type						
	1	2	3	4	5	6	7
C	V	III	II	XII	X	VIII	VII
C#	VI	IV	III	XIII	XI	IX	VIII
D	VII	V	IV	II	XII	X	IX
Eb (D#)	VIII	VI	V	III	I	XI	X
E	IX	VII	VI	IV	II	XII	XI
F	X	VIII	VII	V	III	I	XII
F#	XI	IX	VIII	VI	IV	II	XIII
G	XII	X	IX	VII	V	III	II
G# (Ab)	XIII	XI	X	VIII	VI	IV	III
A	II	XII	XI	IX	VII	V	IV
Bb (A#)	III	I	XII	X	VIII	VI	V
B	IV	II	XIII	XI	IX	VII	VI

Locrian Scale Positions

Key	Fingering Type						
	1	2	3	4	5	6	7
C (B#)	III	I	XII	X	VIII	VI	V
C#	IV	II	XIII	XI	IX	VII	VI
D	V	III	II	XII	X	VIII	VII
D#	VI	IV	III	XIII	XI	IX	VIII
E	VII	V	IV	II	XII	X	IX
F (E#)	VIII	VI	V	III	I	XI	X
F#	IX	VII	VI	IV	II	XII	XI
G	X	VIII	VII	V	III	I	XII
G#	XI	IX	VIII	VI	IV	II	XIII
A	XII	X	IX	VII	V	III	II
A# (Bb)	I	XI	X	VIII	VI	IV	III
B	II	XII	XI	IX	VII	V	IV

Another (and perhaps more practical) way of transposing a modal scale is to think of it as a variation of the parallel major (or natural minor) scale, as follows.

Dorian	Minor scale with raised 6th
Phrygian	Minor scale with lowered 2nd
Lydian	Major scale with raised 4th
Mixolydian	Major scale with lowered 7th
Locrian	Minor scale with lowered 5th and 2nd

If you know your major and minor scale fingerings, you will find it easy to adapt them to play modal scales in this way. For example, to play an F Lydian Scale, use an F major scale with a raised 4th.

F Major, Type 4

F Lydian, Type 4 (modified)

This *parallel* (or *tonic*) method of transposing modes is often easier and quicker than basing the modal scale on its relative major scale fingering. However, it is important to understand both of these methods of transposing modal scales.

The Chromatic Scale

The *chromatic scale* (also known as the *dodecuple scale*) contains all twelve tones in one octave. The chromatic scale is classified as a *symmetrical scale* because it has an even interval between every note—the interval of a half step (or *semitone*). Since the chromatic scale does not have a true tonal center, it is not actually in any particular key. Improvisers use portions of the chromatic scale in a wide variety of musical contexts—especially where melodic embellishments and altered chords are the norm.

The chromatic scale exercise below covers three and one-half octaves—from low E to high C on the twentieth fret. This scale will help you learn to shift positions smoothly across the full length of the fretboard. If you are using an electric or acoustic guitar with a cut-away, it should be relatively easy to play the highest notes of this scale. However, the player with a standard-body acoustic guitar should reposition the thumb to the bottom edge of the neck when playing above the twelfth position.

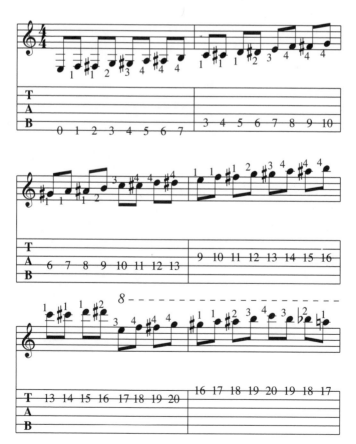

25

Here's another challenging chromatic-scale exercise that involves some swift position changing. Although the position changes every fourth note, you should accent the first note of each triplet group. The exercise is shown here on the B string, but you should practice it on all six strings until you can play it at a moderately fast pace.

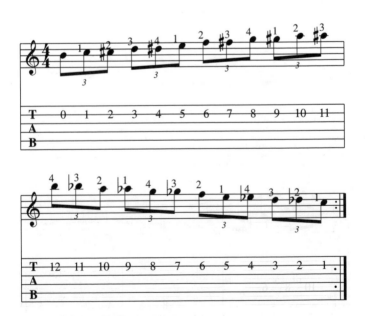

Whole-Tone Scales

As its name implies, a *whole-tone scale* features a whole step interval between notes. Like the chromatic scale, this scale is symmetrical. With six notes per octave, there are actually only two distinct whole-tone scales. Since any note of a whole-tone scale may be considered its root, this type of scale is not associated with a particular key. Improvisers sometimes use portions of the whole-tone scale over an augmented seventh chord (because the scale contains all the tones of the chord plus the alterations 9 and ♯11).

Whole-Tone Scale 1

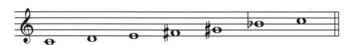

Whole-Tone Scale 2

Play this Whole-Tone Scale 1 exercise now, beginning on a C note. Then try the same exercise up one fret (starting on D♭) to practice Whole-Tone Scale 2.

Tonal Pentatonic Scales

A tonal pentatonic scale is a five-note scale that has no half-tones. The most commonly used scale of this kind is called the *major pentatonic scale*—and is often heard in country and rock music. Note that this scale is based on the major scale (minus the fourth and seventh degrees).

C Major Pentatonic Scale

Four additional pentatonic modes may be derived from the major pentatonic scale by starting on each scale degree in turn. Here's a brief description of the tonal pentatonic modes. These scales occur in the music of many cultures and periods—from the ancient melodies of the Celts, Chinese, and Aztecs to today's most sophisticated rock and jazz improvisations.

Tonal Pentatonic Scale 2. Begins on the second degree of the pentatonic scale. This scale commonly occurs in "old-timey" folk music of the American Southeast. Contemporary bluegrass and country musicians often use this mode to evoke this haunting, traditional sound.

Tonal Pentatonic Scale 3. Begins on the third degree of the major pentatonic scale. Because of its ambiguous tonal center, this unusual scale has limited use.

Tonal Pentatonic Scale 4. Begins on the fourth degree of the pentatonic scale. This form is sometimes considered the "true" tonal pentatonic scale. It occurs in ancient music around the globe, but has limited use in usual contemporary settings. However, it can be heard in avant-garde, new age, and "world" musics that reflect African, Asian, or Celtic influences.

Tonal Pentatonic Scale 5. Also known as the *minor pentatonic scale* (or *pentatonic blues scale*), this form begins on the fifth degree of the major pentatonic scale. This scale is the basis for most traditional blues music—and naturally occurs in today's blues-based jazz and rock. This scale (along with its six-note and seven-note forms) is discussed more fully in the section "Blues Scale Variations."

D Tonal Pentatonic Scale 2

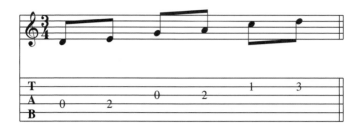

E Tonal Pentatonic Scale 3

G Tonal Pentatonic Scale 4

A Tonal Pentatonic Scale 5
(also known as Minor Pentatonic *or* Pentatonic Blues*)*

Because the tonal pentatonic scales may be used with a wide variety of chords and progressions, they allow for a good deal of melodic freedom. For this reason, modern songwriters and improvisers use these scales to evoke a powerful ethnic or avant-garde sound, particularly in an alternative jazz or new age context. Once you are familiar with the above scales, explore the modes derived from another major pentatonic scale in a different key, such as A or D.

You can derive fingerings for pentatonic scales from basic major-scale patterns. To play a major pentatonic scale, just leave out the fourth and seventh degrees of the parallel major scale fingering pattern. This fingering may also be used to play the four modes of the major pentatonic scale by starting on each scale degree in turn. Here are the four most useful fingerings for tonal pentatonic scales (based on major-scale fingering Types 1, 2, 5, and 6, respectively).

Type 1

Type 2

Type 5

Type 6

Semitonal Pentatonic Scales

A *semitonal pentatonic scale* is a five-note scale that includes half steps. Technically there are two such scales. The first one is produced by omitting the second and sixth degree of the major scale.

C Semitonal Pentatonic Scale

Like the tonal pentatonic scale, this semitonal pentatonic scale has four "modes," as shown.

E Semitonal Pentatonic Scale 2

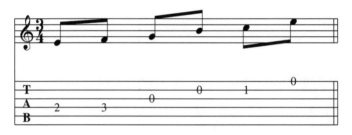

F Semitonal Pentatonic Scale 3

G Semitonal Pentatonic Scale 4

B Semitonal Pentatonic Scale 5

Fingering patterns for semitonal pentatonic scales may be derived from major-scale fingerings. So, to produce the first semitonal pentatonic scale given above, omit the second and sixth degrees of the parallel major scale. This fingering may also be used to play the four modes of this scale by starting on each scale degree in turn. (As with tonal pentatonic scales, the four fingering types which work best for semitonal pentatonic scales are based on major-scale fingering Types 1, 2, 5, and 6.)

The second (or alternate) form of semitonal pentatonic scale is produced by omitting the second and fifth degrees of the major scale. Once you are familiar with this scale, try playing its four modes by beginning on each scale degree in turn.

C Semitonal Pentatonic Scale (Alternate)

As a general rule, semitonal pentatonic scales add a strong dissonant flavor to guitar solos and arrangements. These unusual scales (and their variations) are usually associated with the musics of specific cultures. For this reason, their harmonic applications depend upon their idiomatic contexts—and can not be discussed in general terms.

Several more interesting semitonal pentatonic scales are included in the section "Ethnic Scales" at the end of this book.

Blues Scale Variations

The six-note blues scale (or *major blues scale*) below is based on the major pentatonic scale (with an added ♭3). The presence of a ♮3 in this blues scale gives it a "major sound."

C "Major" Six-Note Blues Scale

As with pentatonic scales, the four fingering types which work best for six-note (or *hexatonic*) blues scales are based on major-scale fingering Types 1, 2, 5, and 6, as shown.

Type 1

Type 2

Type 5

Type 6

Here is another popular six-note blues scale, which is formed by adding a ♭5 to the standard minor pentatonic scale. This "minor" blues scale contains the same notes as the scale above and is considered its relative minor.

A "Minor" Six-Note Blues Scale

To play this scale in any key, start on the sixth degree of the relative major blues scale and apply the same fingering. Try this now using the four fingering patterns above to play A, B, E, and F♯ "minor" six-note blues scales.

The *seven-note blues scale* is another popular variation that is commonly heard in blues, jazz, and rock settings. This scale contains elements of both the "major" and "minor" six-note blues scales previously shown. With all three "blue" notes plus ♮3, this scale is favorite choice of many improvisers.

C Seven-Note Blues Scale

Play this C seven-note blues scale exercise, which incorporates patterns derived from E♭ major-scale fingering Types 2, 1, 6, and 5. It is a common practice to reverse the second and third degrees of this scale when descending, as shown in this example.

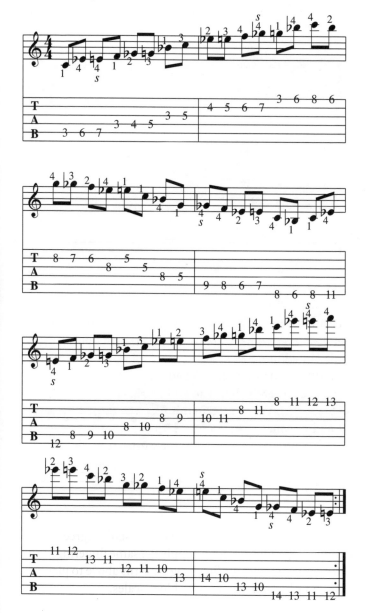

Diminished Scales

The *diminished scale* is commonly used in jazz and classical music—and sometimes also occurs in pop and rock. This scale features a regular alternating pattern of whole-step and half-step intervals. Since every other note of the diminished scale may be considered its root (or tonic), there are only three unique diminished scales.

C Diminished Scale

C♯ Diminished Scale

D Diminished Scale

Because a diminished scale features an equal interval between every other note, it is considered a symmetrical scale. In addition to being used to solo over diminished seventh chords, the diminished scale is often used over dominant seventh chords to add tensions (such as ♭9, ♯9, ♯11, and 13). When used in this way, the root of the scale should be one half-step above the root of the seventh chord. Thus, a C diminished scale works with a B7 chord.

Because of its unusual structure, the diminished scale has many useful fingerings. Here is an interesting pattern that shifts from third to second position, and then back again.

This alternate fingering employs stretches up and down which allow you to remain in one position.

Altered Scales

The *altered scale* is commonly heard in jazz and progressive rock music. This scale may be viewed as a combination of the first half of the diminished scale with the second half of the whole-tone scale, as shown. (Note that the diminished scale used is one half-step higher than the whole-tone scale portion.)

Improvisers use the altered scale over altered dominant chords—that is, dominant seventh chords with the alterations ♭5, ♯5, ♭9, ♯9, and/or ♯11. Play this two-octave altered-scale pattern now in first position.

You'll need to shift positions in the middle of this exercise, which features two additional fingering patterns.

Harmonic Minor Scales

You are already familiar with the natural minor (or Aeolian) scale, discussed previously. In this section, you'll get a chance to practice the *harmonic minor scale*, which is the same as a natural minor scale with a raised 7th. Like other minor scales, the harmonic minor is built on the sixth degree of the corresponding relative major scale. Thus, the A harmonic minor scale is considered to be a relative minor of C major.

The harmonic minor scale is frequently used in heavy metal and modern rock music—and also occurs in various Slavic and Near Eastern folk musics. In jazz, this scale is used more specifically for soloing over the V7 chord in minor keys. When used in this way, the root of the scale should be a fifth below the V7 chord. Thus, a jazz player might use an A harmonic minor scale to solo over an E7b9 chord.

Try this harmonic minor scale exercise now in the key of D minor. Note that this particular scale pattern uses the Aeolian mode of major-scale fingering Type 4 (with a raised 7th).

Once you are familiar with this scale, try adapting other major-scale fingering types to play harmonic minor scales in different keys and positions. (You may want to refer to pages 23 and 24 if you need to review Aeolian scale positions and fingerings.)

Jazz Melodic Minor Scales

As its name implies, the *jazz melodic minor scale* is a variation of the melodic minor scale commonly used in traditional and modern jazz music. As compared to the major scale, the standard melodic minor scale features a lowered 3rd when ascending—and a lowered 3rd, 6th, and 7th when descending. The jazz melodic minor simply uses the ascending melodic minor form for both ascending and descending passages.

Composers and improvisers use the jazz melodic minor scale to construct melodies and solo riffs in a wide range of minor contexts. Here is a D jazz melodic minor scale based on the Aeolian mode of major-scale fingering Type 4. Compare this pattern with the harmonic minor scale in the previous section. Then try adapting other Aeolian fingering patterns to play jazz melodic minor scales in other keys and positions.

Lydian Flat-Seven Scales

You are already familiar with the Lydian scale, which is built on the fourth degree of the major scale. The *Lydian flat-seven scale* is a useful variation commonly heard in jazz music. As its name implies, this scale is formed by lowering the 7th degree of the Lydian scale. (It may also be viewed as the "Lydian mode" of the jazz melodic minor scale, discussed in the previous section.)

Jazz players often use the Lydian flat-seven scale when soloing over dominant seventh chords (although they often switch to the related Mixolydian scale over V7—the true dominant seventh chord). Now try playing this Lydian flat-seven scale pattern using major-scale fingering Type 4 (with a raised 4th and lowered 7th). Then try adapting other major-scale fingering types to play Lydian flat-seven scales in different keys and positions.

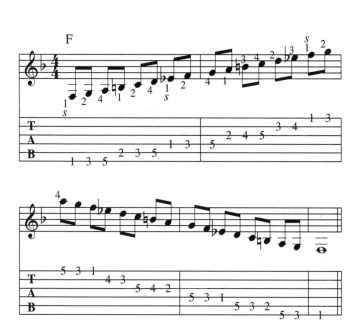

Open-String Scales

Open strings create deep, natural-sounding tones which show off the guitar's resonant quality to its full advantage. For this reason, guitarists sometimes choose open-string scale forms, particularly for arrangements that call for a powerful and resonant sound.

By nature, open-string scales are not moveable. The scales that can be played in this way are limited by the fixed pitches of the instrument's open strings. Because of this limitation, there are comparatively few practical open-string scale patterns.

Since the fingerings for open-string scales are a bit more difficult than the usual positions, it really pays to practice them. If you play fingerstyle, you should have no trouble following the fingering indications (*p*=thumb, *i*=index, *m*=middle, *a*=ring). Pick-style players should use alternating pick and fingers, as shown.

Below are several typical open-string patterns for scales you have learned in previous sections of this book. Practice these examples, and then try coming up with your own open-string patterns.

Remember that the major and pentatonic scale fingerings may also be applied to the modes of the keys in which they are shown. For example, the D major pattern may also be used for an A Mixolydian or E Dorian scale—and the G major pentatonic fingering may be used for an E minor pentatonic blues scale.

D Major Open-String Scale

G Major Pentatonic Open-String Scale

E Aeolian Open-String Scale

A Minor Pentatonic Open-String Scale

G Whole-Tone Open-String Scale

Tap-On Scales

A *tap-on* is basically a hammeron that is played with a finger of the picking hand. Most guitarists use the middle finger for tapping (indicated by a *T*). A tap-on is usually followed by a pulloff to the note below. This tap-on/pulloff sequence is then followed by another pulloff performed by the fretting hand. The resulting three-note pattern gives a triplet feel to tap-on riffs and scales. If you are interested in mastering this interesting technique, it really pays to practice scales that incorporate tap-ons in sequence. Below are two typical tap-on patterns for scales you have learned in previous sections of this book. Practice these examples, and then try coming up with your own tap-on patterns.

G Major Tap-On Scale

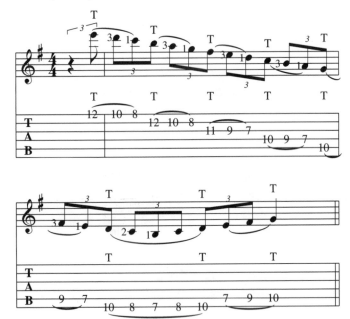

G Harmonic Minor Tap-On Scale

Scales Using Harmonics

Harmonics are often used in a solo context to evoke a haunting or introspective quality. Here is a G major pentatonic scale which will help you build your harmonic chops. This scale uses all natural harmonics played at the twelfth fret.

G Major Pentatonic Scale With Harmonics

You can play this scale in other keys by barring at any fret and using *artificial harmonics*. To play an artificial harmonic, lightly touch the string with the tip of the extended index finger of your picking hand at the point twelve frets above the fretted note. Then pluck the string with your thumb to sound the octave harmonic. Here are three more scales using artificial harmonics.

D Minor Pentatonic Scale With Harmonics

E Semitonal Pentatonic Scale With Harmonics

C Major Scale With Harmonics

Ethnic Scales

Many contemporary guitarists and composers have found inspiration by exploring the scales of other cultures, particularly those of the Eastern Hemisphere. You have already learned many important ethnic scales in previous sections of this book. For instance, tonal and semitonal pentatonic scales are found in the music of diverse ancient and modern cultures, from the native tribes of America and Africa to Indonesia and the Far East.

In this section, you will find additional ethnic scales which feature interesting "non-diatonic" harmonies. Certain of these scales traditionally feature microtonal harmonies which have here been interpreted for use with the standard guitar tuning. Although these scales may sound inappropriate in traditional settings, they can be very effective in contemporary new age and "world" music contexts.

Gypsy Minor Scale

The *Gypsy minor scale* (also called *Hungarian minor*) features a lowered 3rd and 6th, and a raised 4th. It may also be viewed as a harmonic minor scale with a raised 4th. This distinctive scale is common in the folk music of Eastern Europe and occurs in contemporary Turkish and Jewish music as well. During the 19th and 20th centuries, Béla Bartók and other composers devoted much attention to this interesting scale and its applications in contemporary classical music.

Neapolitan Minor Scale

The *Neapolitan minor scale* features a lowered 2nd, 3rd, and 6th degree—and may also be viewed as a harmonic minor scale with a lowered 2nd. This scale is identified with the *Neapolitan School*, a term loosely applied to an Italian style of composition popular in the 18th century.

Japanese Scales

Hirajoshi Scale

Kumoi Scale

In Scale

African Scales

Tanzanian Scale

Congolese Scale

Indian Scales

Bhairava Scale

Pooravi Scale

Marava Scale

Kanakangi Scale

Balinese Scale

Pelog Scale